CU00690579

Late Georgian and Regency Furniture

Christopher Gilbert

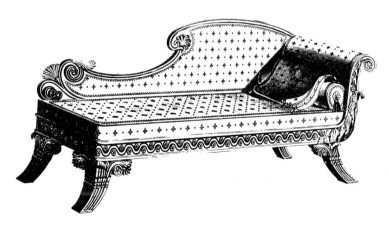

COUNTRY LIFE COLLECTORS' GUIDES

Sheraton style secrétaire cabinet in mahogany and satinwood with writing and dressing drawers containing silver fitments hallmarked 1799. About 1800. Temple Newsam House, Leeds.

An Introduction to Furniture

Numbers in the margin refer to the page where an illustration may be found

The most rewarding approach to fine antique furniture of any period involves close study of many interrelated factors, and the following introductory notes have been framed to assist those who wish to develop a broad knowledge of the subject. The chapters which follow deal specifically with late Georgian and Regency furniture.

Firstly, one should attempt to define the materials of which a piece is made. The more common timbers such as oak, walnut, mahogany, satinwood, rosewood and pine are quite easy to recognise, but some native woods used by specialist craftsmen or in country districts–chestnut, ash, lime, cherry or yew for example–are more difficult, while confident identification of the many exotic woods popular during the late 18th century for

30 elaborate **marquetry** designs (especially if scorched or stained to enhance their decorative effect) requires considerable expertise. In practice the ability to recognise various timbers is simplified because English craftsmen worked within a slowly

2, 4 evolving tradition in which their **choice of wood** was largely dictated by its technical or visual qualities. For instance, beech was commonly used for late Georgian painted chair frames, box or holly for white inlaid stringing lines, pine for carved and gilt mirrors, tulipwood for crossbanding and native timbers for

16, 61 routine **country-made furniture**. An obvious way to train one's eye is by visiting museums of decorative art such as the Wallace Collection and Victoria and Albert in London, or Temple Newsam,

Leeds, and the Bowes Museum, Barnard Castle, where the various timbers are named on labels.

Of course many secondary materials were employed by furniture-makers and these possess the same kind of interest as wood. Bone, **ivory**, mother-of-pearl, **brass**, pewter and tortoiseshell were used to embellish cabinetwork together with ceramic plaques, rich **ormolu mounts** and **silver fitments**. Panels of **tooled leather** and colourful **marble slabs** feature on table tops while cast iron, papier-mâché and even horn were sometimes used instead of timber. All these mediums repay careful study for they represent the work of specialist craftsmen who participated in the production of furniture.

5, 49

25, 2
20, 26

Sheraton style work box on stand in satinwood inlaid with walnut and box. About 1795. Temple Newsam House, Leeds.

In the 18th century many leading firms combined the trades of cabinetmaker and upholsterer, and contemporary accounts
57 show that luxurious **bed hangings**, chair covers and screen panels were often vastly more expensive than the supporting frames. Furnishing textiles provide an immensely interesting field of enquiry although naturally the original fabrics have often been renewed.

The finest Georgian furniture combines the use of carefully selected materials with a high technical finish and it is important to cultivate the ability to distinguish between various grades of timber and levels of craftsmanship. Examination of the joints uniting separate members of a chair or the carcass of cabinetwork

Spinning wheel bearing the trade label of John Planta, Fulneck, near Leeds. Mahogany with ivory fitments and a metal wheel. About 1800. Temple Newsam House, Leeds.

gives a valuable insight into the basic quality of a piece, for the hidden parts of furniture should be neatly and cleanly finished off. The finesse with which drawer linings have been constructed 6 (particularly the **dovetailing**) is most instructive and the execu- 6 tion of **mortice and tenon**, **tongue and groove**, and **mitred** joints provides a similar indication of quality.

Having appraised the basic structure the various decorative processes must be assessed. Skilled carving will be crisp and confident while inferior work appears flat and lifeless; the 30 technique of **marquetry** decoration involves a complicated series of delicate operations and the best examples display much greater refinement than routine work. One should likewise be able to recognise a well cut moulding, carefully controlled **turned** 34, 7 **ornament**, expert **crossbanding** and similar hallmarks of 7, 29, 19 calibre. Metal mounts, **painted designs**, **gilding**, **japanning** (imitation oriental lacquer) and various other decorative treat-

Some typical joints. The execution of joints is an indication of quality.

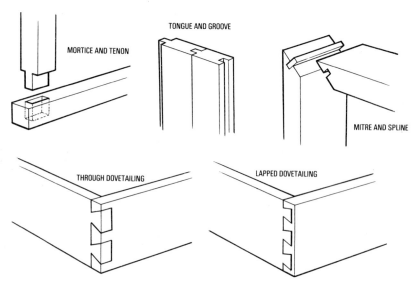

MORTICE AND TENON

TONGUE AND GROOVE

MITRE AND SPLINE

THROUGH DOVETAILING

LAPPED DOVETAILING

Sheraton style Harlequin Pembroke table in satinwood and mahogany with painted decoration and crossbanded borders. The central till lowers into the deep framing. About 1790. Temple Newsam House, Leeds.

ments also have to be judged when evaluating furniture. Connoisseurship can only flow from direct experience of handling antiques; one should therefore seek every opportunity to examine authentic work in shops, the sale room, and private or public collections. Careful observation of the construction, craftsmanship, surface condition, colour, evidence of wear etc. deepens one's understanding of ageing processes and serves to reveal whether a piece has been altered at any time or is possibly a competent reproduction.

Metal handles, castors, hinges and locks should always be scrutinised because these fitments are prone to damage and are frequently renewed. Many handsome Sheraton-style chests of drawers were originally equipped with simple wooden knobs, but owing to modern prejudice against this type of handle they are frequently replaced by flashy reproduction brass sets. Late Georgian locks are occasionally stamped with the name of a
43, 62 patentee such as **I. Bramah**, **Stubbs** or Barron. The signature on a lock may be accompanied by the initials of the reigning monarch G. R., W. R., or V. R. beneath a crown, and this device provides a useful guide to dating furniture made during the 1820s and 1830s. The practice of marking became more general in the mid 19th century and, since locks on early cabinet furniture were often replaced with improved models, signed examples, unless original, can be misleading. Brass hinges, castors and bolts were also supplied by specialists, but few early signed examples have been noted.

During the late Georgian period decorative styles were continuously being modified by the demands of fashion and it is often possible to date furniture solely on stylistic grounds to within about five years, although naturally some firms were more conservative than others and the work of provincial makers tended to be traditional in character. Through studying **en-**
9 **graved designs** and tracing documented furniture, art historians have established very accurately when particular design types and decorative motifs were in vogue. The monumental three-volume *Dictionary of English Furniture* by Ralph Edwards illustrates thousands of typical examples, each of which has been

exactly dated. Almost any piece of antique domestic furniture can be accurately placed within its chronological framework and on the evidence of stylistic analogy given an approximate date. It should be stressed that when dating a piece it is imperative to look for the *latest* stylistic feature and remember that if the character indicates a provincial origin it will probably be rather later than a similar object made in London.

English furniture-makers have never been required by law to mark their work and prior to the Victorian era very few practised this form of advertisement; consequently most antique furniture is anonymous. Leading firms depended for commissions mainly on the personal recommendation of satisfied clients and architects, although trade cards were occasionally fixed to certain pieces. Provincial firms had fewer reservations about using a maker's mark although signed items are by no means common.

Detail of medallion.

Engraved design for a sconce for Derby House.
Robert Adam. About 1774.

After about 1780 **Gillows of Lancaster** started to impress their name on furniture, the stamp being placed unobtrusively on for instance the front edge of a drawer, the seat rail or back leg of a chair or the underframe of a table. Some firms adopted the alternative method of pasting **printed labels** on to their products but this technique was less permanent and many must have disappeared; one should, incidentally, beware of labels which have been surreptitiously removed from a minor or damaged piece and stuck on to a more saleable article.

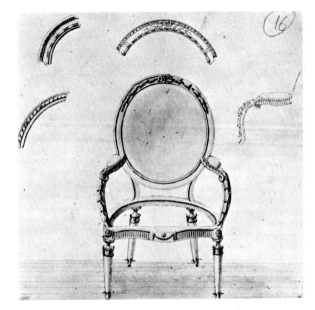

right Design for an armchair. Thomas Chippendale. Pen and grey wash. 8 in × 7 in. Collection of Mr and Mrs J. Chichester-Constable, Burton Constable, Yorkshire.

opposite Mahogany chair. The splat corresponds closely to a design in Chippendale's *Director.* About 1755–1760. Temple Newsam House, Leeds.

If one is lucky enough to discover a piece of marked furniture, information about the maker may be recorded in Sir Ambrose Heal's *London Furniture Makers 1660–1840,* but virtually the only way of obtaining details about provincial firms is through consulting old Trade Directories. This source is particularly helpful in the case of labelled 19th-century pieces when both the name and address is recorded.

Following the appearance in 1754 of Thomas Chippendale's famous *Gentleman and Cabinet-Maker's Director* containing engraved designs for household furniture, several London firms issued similar catalogues. The most influential of these are now available in facsimile editions, therefore it is not difficult to establish whether a piece of furniture is **based on a published design**. However, since the majority of **pattern books** were bought by cabinetmakers who wished to keep abreast of fashion, even exact correspondence does not prove that an item was made by the person who issued the design. Nevertheless, it is always satisfying to find a piece which conforms to a contemporary engraving.

10

17, 28, 40, 50

Most furniture-makers conceived and executed their own work; therefore if an article is based on an unpublished drawing by a cabinetmaker it can be assumed that the author or his firm was responsible for both. For instance, collections of drawings by Matthias Lock and John Linnell at the Victoria and Albert Museum permit the attribution of several otherwise undocumented pieces to these masters, and the Burton Constable papers include some **signed designs** which reveal the author of furniture preserved in the house.

11

It is always worth investigating the former history of furniture, because many important country house collections have been dispersed since the last war and the interest of pieces is greatly enhanced if they are known to have come from a stately home furnished by a well known patron of the arts. Once the provenance has been elucidated it may be possible to trace an illustrated article in *Country Life* portraying the object in its original setting and revealing if it once formed part of a larger suite. In exceptional cases where documentation exists one can identify pieces in old inventories and even–the ultimate triumph–trace the original bill. Many landed families have deposited their papers in County Record Offices and such archives generally include furniture accounts. At present few private collectors or dealers appreciate the significance of documented furniture and seldom attempt to clarify the history even of outstanding items, but this evidence should in the interests of scholarship be sought and fully recorded, for it will inevitably be more difficult to obtain in the future.

Furniture, in common with contemporary letters, diaries, novels and conversation pictures reveals much about the social life of the past. Breakfast tables are for instance a document of the period when it was fashionable to rise late and breakfast upstairs, port tables fitted with travelling coasters and a fire screen were admirably attuned to the needs of masculine drinking parties and tribes of shaving tables and basin stands survive from an age when private bathrooms were unknown. Furniture therefore reflects a way of life and can be enjoyed as visible social history.

The Rococo, Chinese and Gothic Styles

Throughout the 18th century English furniture was profoundly influenced by continental fashions; we in Britain have nearly always received impulses from abroad and seldom projected a national style. In 1760 an anglicised version of the French *rocaille* style dominated the decorative arts in this country. It had been formulated by such designers as Jean Berain, Nicolas Pineau and Meissonier and was first assimilated by English silversmiths in the 1730s. The style was not taken up by furniture-makers until the following decade and only achieved popularity after the publication in 1754 of Chippendale's *Director*. However, the majority of English architects continued to work in the Palladian tradition and Rococo never quite attained the status of a truly national style.

The dignified 'logically articulated' conventions which ruled furniture design during the pre-*Director* period were discarded in favour of a curvilinear, asymmetrical and often frivolous system of surface ornament inspired by natural plant forms instead of Palladian architecture. In France the Rococo movement had evolved slowly over several decades, but English furniture-makers were compelled to annex the style in its mature form before they fully understood its capabilities. Accordingly, their work rarely displays the self-confident flamboyance or subtleties of French prototypes. Many of the spectacular **Rococo designs** published for the benefit of carvers and gilders were reinterpreted by the craftsmen in simpler terms and invested with a typically English restraint.

17

13

The revolutionary new style was characterised by a bold use of
serpentine lines embracing the whole design. At its most ac-
complished, Rococo furniture conveys the impression of rhyth-
mic curvelinear movement, of asymmetry with no loss of balance,
poised exuberance and picturesque charm. The flowing structural
lines were delicately embellished with playful C-scrolls and a
wide repertory of decorative motifs derived from nature such as
flowers, foliage, **tree-forms**, animals, bulrushes, sea shells, rock-
work, **stalactite concretions**, flames, falling water and similar
fantastic elements. It has been suggested that many of these weird
features were inspired by the interiors of grottoes. It was found
that the Rococo idiom was admirably suited to mirror frames, console tables, sconces, chandeliers and **stands** which offered un-
limited scope for virile carving, but English makers were less
assured than the French in applying the style to case furniture
and chair frames. The more far-fetched designs for such pieces
were generally simplified by craftsmen who attempted to execute
them, although **chair backs** did provide an opportunity for
fanciful elaboration.

The first English designer to master the Rococo was the carver and engraver Matthias Lock who published *Six Sconces*, *Six Tables*, and *A New Book of Ornament* between 1744 and 1752. These designs together with an album of highly proficient drawings indicate that he was one of the earliest exponents of the new fashion. There is evidence that Lock worked for Thomas Chippendale during the 1750s and early 1760s; it is therefore likely that he encouraged his employer to exploit the Rococo style. Chippendale was a successful young business man who had been trained as a cabinetmaker and almost certainly received instruction at one of the St Martin's Lane drawing schools where Hubert Gravelot, the well known designer, taught. When Chippendale's *Director* appeared in 1754, it contained one hundred and sixty engraved plates portraying a comprehensive range of household

opposite Mahogany commode with bronze handles. Restrained *Director* style. About 1755–1760. Temple Newsam House, Leeds.

Rococo candlestand in carved pine with metal branches. About 1760. Based on a design published by Thomas Johnson in 1758. One of four formerly at Hagley Hall, Worcestershire. Temple Newsam House, Leeds.

Oak table in
Country
Chippendale
style. About
1770. Private
collection.

furniture in the Rococo, Gothic and Chinese styles. This volume
was in such demand that a reprint was issued the following year
and the designs rapidly became accepted as a fashionable norm.
It exerted such a powerful influence on contemporary taste that
the generic term **'Chippendale'** is now indiscriminately used to
describe any piece of mid 18th-century furniture which broadly
corresponds to the style of plates in the *Director*. The ensuing
publicity undoubtedly stimulated business, for all Chippendale's
known commissions date from after its publication (see *Chippendale*, by E.T. Joy, in this series).

The success of this venture inspired other firms to produce
similar trade catalogues in which the development of the Rococo
style can be traced. Between 1755 and 1761 the carver and gilder
Thomas Johnson issued sets of engravings for **girandoles**,
console tables, mirrors, **stands** and chimneypieces in the most
advanced Rococo idiom. His linear designs were more spiky,
restless and extravagant than Chippendale's and he often introduced picturesque rustic figures, beasts and **contorted trees**
into his vigorously executed compositions. The revised edition
of Chippendale's *Director* published in 1762 reveals a distinct

10, 14, 17

15, 17

15

17

movement towards this wild and whimsical style which characterised the final phase of the movement in England. The firm of Ince & Mayhew also brought out a book of furniture designs in emulation of Chippendale entitled *The Universal System of Household Furniture* containing one hundred plates exemplifying their own brand of Rococo ornament, and the cabinet- and chairmaker Robert Manwering included a number of degenerate Rococo designs in three books published in 1765 and 1766.

Although engraved designs are a source of great interest to furniture historians, it must be remembered that the majority of firms never entertained this kind of publicity, although large concerns undoubtedly employed skilled draughtsmen. Carefully executed designs would normally be submitted to a patron for approval before a commission was started, and instructive collec-

Design for a Rococo girandole from Thomas Johnson's *Collection of Designs* (1758), Plate LI.

Mahogany armchair in Chinese Chippendale style, the top rail carved with the crest of Connock. About 1760. Formerly at Treworgey Manor Cornwall. Temple Newsam House, Leeds.

tions of such drawings by Lock and Linnell have been preserved.

17, 40, 50 **Pattern books** served to popularise new styles, the designs rarely being slavishly copied even by the authors. Nor did they function as illustrated trade catalogues from which customers could order directly; they were intended rather to advertise the general capabilities of a firm and assist other furniture makers as a useful magazine of fashionable design types and decorative treatments.

The arts of China have periodically bemused Europeans. The taste for chinoiserie first assumed the proportions of a fashionable craze during the late 17th century when blue-and-white porcelain was avidly collected, and imported panels of lacquer extensively used in the construction of cabinets and screens. During the early Georgian period the popularity of chinoiserie decreased, but towards the middle of the century designers once again drew inspiration from oriental sources and **pseudo-**
17 **Chinese motifs were freely blended with Rococo ornament**.

Although Thomas Chippendale's designs were not the first manifestations of this revival, the *Director* displays the earliest skilful synthesis of the new wave of decorative ideas. No attempt was made to reproduce actual examples of Chinese furniture; instead, certain picturesque features derived from illustrated travel books or scenes on imported porcelain, paper hangings and so forth were fancifully combined with traditional English
19 elements. The upward swish of **pagoda roofs** was effectively used as a cresting for cabinets, mirrors, hanging shelves and beds,
17 the interlocking staggered squares of **Chinese lattice paling** were adopted for rectangular chair backs, glazing bars and as a pattern for ubiquitous open and blind frets. Other popular motifs included simulated bamboo, mandarins perched on delightful
19 **bell-hung** temples, fantastic ho-ho birds, dragons and similar
19 eye-catching trivia. A certain amount of **japanned** furniture was also made; in 1759 Chippendale supplied a 'Jappan'd Cloaths-press wt folding doors and sliding shelves' to the Earl of Dumfries.

Although critics of the new-fangled taste denounced it as 'barbarous and frivolous' Thomas Johnson's *One Hundred and Fifty New Designs* published in 1761, the third edition of the

Director issued the following year, and other pattern books indicate that the vogue flourished well into the 1760s. There is, however, some evidence that it was increasingly relegated to the less formal regions of fashionable houses such as bed- and dressing-rooms. In 1787 Sir William Chambers, one of the leading architects, attempted to 'put a stop to the extravagancies that daily appear under the name of Chinese' by issuing a volume entitled *Designs of Chinese Buildings, Furniture etc.* which accurately portrayed various pieces of oriental furniture which he had drawn during a visit to Canton. His designs lacked the frivolity and charm of those conceived by his contemporaries who had no first-hand experience of China and they exerted little influence

China stand in the Chinese taste, japanned in red, black and gold. About 1755. Formerly at Badminton House. Lady Lever Art Gallery, Port Sunlight, Cheshire.

on current fashion, but as replicas they served to show how whimsical were the chinoiserie fabrications of other designers.

The Chinese style is sometimes found in association with Gothic elements – both themes formed tributaries of the Rococo movement – although the **mid 18th-century Gothic Revival**, unlike the cult for chinoiserie, was exclusive to England. Interest in medieval buildings was encouraged during the 1740s by collections of designs such as Batty Langley's *Gothic Architecture Improved* (1742) and received powerful stimulus from the amateur architect and dilettante Horace Walpole, who between 1747 and 1753 decorated and furnished his villa at Strawberry Hill in Neo-Gothic taste. Another leading exponent was the gentleman architect, Sanderson Miller; a **library table** of pronounced Gothic

20, 21, 22

20

Mahogany library writing table in Gothic style. About 1760. Made for the Earl of Pomfret's Neo-Gothic house built by Sanderson Miller in Arlington Street, London. Temple Newsam House, Leeds.

opposite Detail of Gothic ornament on one pedestal of the table (see below).

character now at Temple Newsam, Leeds, was made for a mock-medieval house in Arlington Street, London, which he built for Lady Pomfret in 1760.

Chippendale was the first to publish sophisticated designs for furniture exploiting the new style, and his *Director* engravings played an important part in promoting and sustaining the fashion which persisted until the mid 1760s. No attempt was made to simulate authentic medieval furniture and few patrons even insisted that the repertoire of Gothic ornament be consistently applied. Instead, a hybrid style emerged in which Rococo and Gothic themes, sometimes blended with Chinese elements, co-existed. Picturesque details derived from ecclesiastical architecture were grafted on to pieces which otherwise conformed to

Mahogany chair inlaid with brass strings. About 1760. The pointed tracery and clustered columns combined with standard mid 18th-century ornament are typical of Gothic Revival furniture. Temple Newsam House, Leeds.

standard mid 18th-century types. Features such as **clustered** 22, 20 **columns**, **delicate tracery**, finials, crockets, ogees, **cusps** and pretty frets based on stone friezes were artistically used to embellish all kinds of domestic furniture. Owing to its antiquarian associations the style was particularly favoured for libraries; accordingly bookcases, reading desks, and library tables frequently convey a vivid impression of the style. The **backs of** 22 **chairs** also provided scope for fanciful Gothic treatment and many of Chippendale's elaborately carved mirror frames were composed of a synthesis of Rococo, Chinese and Gothic ingredients.

Although it was not as rife as the parallel Chinese cult, 'Strawberry Hill Gothic' forms an intriguing episode in the history of taste, for it scarcely influenced the design of silver and china and never spread to the continent.

The Neo-classical Revival

Between about 1765 and 1770 fashionable taste was revolutionised by the Neo-classical movement which commanded an im-
mense source of new decorative ideas derived from classical
antiquity. Interest in ancient sites had been roused by the current
excavation of the buried cities of Herculaneum and Pompeii and
sustained by the publication of lavish volumes containing accurate engravings of decorative remains such as Stuart and
Revett's *Antiquities of Athens* (1762), Robert Wood on *Baalbeck
and Palmyra* and Sir William Hamilton's *Etruscan, Greek and
Roman Antiquities*, together with Piranesi's etchings, all of which
provided designers with a ready source of adaptable shapes and
motifs.

The architect Robert Adam, who became the leading exponent
of the Neo-classical style, spent three years in Italy cultivating
a knowledge of ancient sites, notably the Baths of Diocletian and
Hadrian's Villa at Tivoli. He returned to England in 1758 with an
intense enthusiasm for ancient art and an ambition to emulate
'the beautiful spirit of antiquity and transfuse it with novelty
and variety'.

A generation earlier William Kent had evolved a style of interior decoration and furniture design based on the work of
16th-century interpreters of classical buildings such as Palladio,
Serlio and Inigo Jones. Robert Adam's decorative schemes were
on the other hand founded on a direct historical approach to

antiquity and conformed more nearly to the spirit of classical originals. However, he was not concerned merely to imitate ancient interiors but used them as a source of inspiration in expressing his own **personal version of classical beauty**.

24

In contrast to the exuberance of Rococo, the Neo-classical style was imbued with formal, refined qualities and ushered in a completely new array of light and delicate surface ornaments: **honeysuckle motifs, urns, paterae, festoons of husks, medallions** enclosing classical figures, palm-leaves, **rams' heads** and **scrolls of foliage** arranged in graceful patterns.

9, 24, 27
25
25

In 1759–1760 Adam secured his first important commission, the decoration and furnishing of Kedleston Hall, Derbyshire, in the antique style, and in 1761 he produced plans for remodelling the interior of Syon House for the Duke of Northumberland, undertakings which established his reputation and within a brief time revolutionised English taste. As his admirer Sir John Soane observed, 'The light and elegant ornaments imitated from the ancient works in the Baths and Villas of the Romans were soon applied in designs for chairs, tables, carpets and in every other species of furniture.'

Adam invariably sought to create an impression of stylistic harmony between the 'delicacy, gaiety, grace and beauty' of his decorative schemes and the moveables. However, although he had studied Roman domestic interiors at Herculaneum and Pompeii, very few specimens of ancient furniture were actually known, and in the absence of models he was compelled to invent his own classical designs. Initially he experimented with grafting the new repertoire of antique ornament on to restrained Rococo forms or combining it with the architectural style favoured by William Kent, but through constant refinement and improvement he developed a highly original idiom. Adam was chiefly concerned with designs for wall furniture such as mirrors, **side tables**, **sconces** and **commodes** or decorative objects (stands, tripods and pedestals) which featured prominently in his interior schemes. One of his most successful innovations was the dining-room sideboard flanked by **pedestals with urns** and a wine cooler beneath. Much of this display furniture was **painted** or

26, 9, 24

27

24

opposite Design for a commode with painted decoration and ormolu mounts in the Neo-classical taste. Robert Adam, 1771. Sir John Soane's Museum, London.

right Detail of cabinetwork and ormolu mounts on the Neo-classical library table made by Thomas Chippendale for Harewood House, Yorkshire. About 1771. Temple Newsam House, Leeds.

26 **gilt** although for cabinet pieces he used formal marquetry decoration. In contrast to the flamboyant curves of Rococo a distinctive

26 quality of Adam's style was the use of straight lines, **ovals** and flat surfaces delicately enriched with light mouldings and graceful patterns. By 1775 the Neo-classical style had superseded Chippendale's *Director* style in all but the most rural areas.

The designs for moveables which Adam supplied to his patrons would be executed by the principal firm involved in furnishing

Side table with carved, painted and gilt frame and marble top. About 1775. Made for the tapestry room at Osterley Park to a design by Robert Adam. Osterley Park, Middlesex.

Adam style sideboard pedestal and urn. About 1775. One of a pair, in mahogany with ormolu mounts. The pedestal is fitted as a plate warmer with racks and a tray for charcoal. Temple Newsam House, Leeds.

the house, but since he was only concerned with those pieces directly related to his decorative schemes cabinetmakers were themselves required to design the supporting cast in approved Neo-classical style. For instance William France was employed at Kenwood, John Linnell worked at Kedleston and Chippendale was commissioned to execute Adam's designs for seat furniture at 19 Arlington Street and provided independently a whole range of additional items.

Although Chippendale was among the earliest furniture-makers to adopt the new convention, the revised edition of his *Director* published in 1762 displays little awareness of the impending change in fashion. Lock issued a few designs for pier frames in the Neo-classical taste in 1769 and was followed in 1770 by Matthew Darly, but the first major collection to appear was Adam's own *Works in Architecture* issued in parts between 1773 and 1779.

Adam always ensured that his interiors were equipped only with furniture of the finest quality; therefore many leading firms such as Norman, Linnell, Cobb, Bradburn, Beckwith, France and Chippendale acquired an early introduction to the new style which they handled in their own manner. The development of Chippendale's distinctive version of the Adam style can be traced

Design for a Pembroke
table. George Hepple-
white's *Guide* (1788),
Plate LXII.

in furniture he made for Nostell Priory, **Harewood House**,
Newby Hall, **Burton Constable**, Paxton House and elsewhere.
The Harewood commission (1768–1778), easily the most important of his career, was worth nearly £7,000 and resulted in the
production of what is generally regarded as the finest collection
of marquetry furniture in the Neo-classical style in existence.

During the 1770s the Adam style came to dominate the furniture trade at all levels, generally being translated into vernacular
terms to meet the requirements of a large middle class clientele.
This phase of the movement is well illustrated by the **designs of
George Hepplewhite**, published in 1788 (two years after the
author's death) in a volume titled *The Cabinet-Maker and Upholsterer's Guide or, repository of designs for every article of
household furniture, in the newest and most approved taste*. It
was reissued in 1789 and a revised edition appeared in 1794.
Nothing is known of Hepplewhite's career except that he had
been apprenticed to Gillows of Lancaster and later established a
small business in Cripplegate, London.

The preface discloses that Hepplewhite's aim was 'to unite
elegance and utility and blend the useful with the agreeable' and

Neo-classical armchair in gilt beech from a large drawing-room suite made by Thomas Chippendale for Burton Constable, Yorkshire. About 1774. Collection of Mr and Mrs J. Chichester-Constable. Burton Constable.

Hepplewhite style mahogany card table. About 1780. Temple Newsam House, Leeds.

it is clear from the admission, 'We designedly followed the latest or most prevailing fashion' that the *Guide* was intended to provide a summary of modern taste rather than promote a new style. The representative nature of this collection enhances its interest for it records the range of **ordinary domestic furniture** produced by legions of conservative firms. The routine classical repertoire of urns, husks, anthemion motifs, medallions, paterae, slender square or round tapering legs and enriched flat surfaces are skilfully deployed in a series of simple yet elegant designs. Oval, shield- and **heart-shaped** chair backs, sometimes incorporating the three **Prince of Wales feathers** or wheat-ear motifs, bow-fronted commodes (for which satinwood was recommended if made for 'rooms of consequence') and a number of plain, rather archaic tallboys and clothes presses suggest the range of advanced and more traditional styles current in the 1780s.

Certain designs such as those for formal sideboard units, **commodes** and pier tables with elaborately inlaid or painted decoration are plainly inspired by Adam's work while those for bookcases, presses and other utility cabinet pieces—articles which Adam disregarded—reveal a debt to plates in Chippendale's

Director. However, the bed- and dressing-room furniture, chairs,
28 **occasional tables** and secrétaire cabinets are invested with a
distinctly post-Adam style of elegance. The term French Hepplewhite is generally applied to a class of chairs and stools with
graceful cabriole legs.

In 1788 a trade manual called *The Cabinet-Makers' London
Book of Prices* appeared containing forty designs by Thomas
Shearer (with directions for costing) which Sheraton observed
were 'more fashionable' than Hepplewhite's which 'had already
caught the decline'. They are instructive examples of the kind of
convenient multi-purpose furniture in demand during the late
18th century, and a comparatively large amount of furniture
32 exists displaying broad parallels to **Shearer's engravings**. The
designs are much less highly decorated than those of Hepplewhite
and mark a reaction against the sumptuousness of the early Neo-
classical style.

Commode in harewood with marquetry decoration in the Neo-classical style.
About 1780. Temple Newsam House, Leeds.

The formative influence behind furniture of the 1790s was Thomas Sheraton's widely circulated *Cabinet-Maker and Upholsterer's Drawing Book* issued in parts between 1791 and 1794. It contained 'a variety of original designs for household furniture, in the newest and most elegant style' which differ markedly in spirit from Hepplewhite's work. Sheraton had been trained as a cabinetmaker in Stockton-on-Tees before moving to London about 1790 and setting up as a drawing master; it is therefore unlikely that he ever owned a workshop or executed any pieces conforming to his published engravings.

The designs display certain affinities to refined French furniture of the late Louis XVI and Directoire periods and the influence of Henry Holland who had lately furnished Carlton House for the Prince of Wales is also pervasive. Sheraton was evidently deeply impressed by the apartments which Holland equipped, for he included six views of the principal rooms.

left Hepplewhite style satinwood armchair. About 1785. Temple Newsam House, Leeds.

below Sheraton style mahogany armchair of the square back type. About 1795.

Bow-fronted sideboard in mahogany and satinwood in the style of Thomas Shearer. About 1795. Temple Newsam House, Leeds.

Bow-fronted sideboard in mahogany and satinwood in the style of Thomas Shearer. About 1795. Temple Newsam House, Leeds.

2, 4   Most of Sheraton's designs have a strong **vertical emphasis**
2   conveyed by the use of straight lines, **slender colonnettes**, and
4, 31   **tapering legs** of square section. He preferred square outlines
31   for **chair backs** in contrast to **Hepplewhite** heart- or shield-
shaped patterns and his cabinet pieces display a similar taste
for simple rectangular forms. He also made more sparing use
of Adam's familiar ornamental repertoire than his predecessors,
the Neo-classical element being either greatly diluted or replaced
by delicately painted figure subjects or naturalistic **floral decora-**
7   **tion**. Many designs derive their elegance purely from carefully
2   studied proportions and a skilful use of **stringing lines**, cross-
2, 7   banding and **contrasting veneers** applied in simple geometrical
patterns on large flat or gracefully curved surfaces.

    Over five hundred furniture-makers living in London and the
provinces subscribed to the *Drawing Book* which supplied them
with an unrivalled series of refined and practical designs in the
latest fashionable taste. It is fitting that Sheraton has given his
name to the culminating phase of 18th-century furniture style.

The Regency Period

The word Regency has now superseded the old term Empire to describe English furniture made during the first thirty years of the 19th century, and the label Adelaide is sometimes applied to pieces dating from the short reign of William IV (1830–1837) in honour of his Queen, Adelaide of Saxe-Meiningen. Even this name is rather misleading, for the constitutional Regency only covered nine years (1811–1820) and during its mature phase the style was not advanced by the Prince Regent whose taste is reflected in the gaudy oriental splendours of Brighton Pavilion. He was, however, associated with its early development and sponsored the revival of interest in **chinoiserie**.

46, 47

Several entirely new types of furniture appeared during the first decade of the 19th century, among them a convenient form of writing desk known as a **davenport**; the canterbury, a kind of low rack for storing music books; elegant stands with open shelves designed to hold ornaments or documents called **whatnots**; and **sofa tables**, all of which became popular.

62

58, 34

Nearly all Regency furniture with the exception of chairs and some dining-tables was veneered, generally with dark rosewood, mahogany or richly figured timbers such as calamander, amboyna, maple, satinwood and kingwood when supplies (impeded by the French wars) were obtainable. Chair frames were often painted or stained black, and japanning was frequently employed instead of veneers for furniture in the Chinese taste. Carving was seldom used as a decorative treatment except for

Regency style sofa table in kingwood and rosewood with ormolu lion's-paw feet. Made by J. & A. Semple in 1809. Temple Newsam House, Leeds.

35 picture and **mirror frames**. T. Martin, writing in 1813, stated that there were only thirteen master-carvers and some sixty journeymen in London, observing that 'carving in wood has long been in the background as a branch of the arts'. Finely cast

34 and chased **ormolu mounts** – seen to great advantage against dark rosewood – were preferred to carved decoration, although it did return to favour during the 1820s. On the other hand there was a strong revival in the craft of turning which was widely

34 used to ornament chair and table legs, **stretchers**, columns and supports.

One of the most attractive features of Regency furniture is the

43 popularity of brass inlay. During the early period **simple strings** and sparse patterns of small motifs arranged in bands or clusters occur, but after about 1812 a taste for exceedingly elaborate

49 overall designs, sometimes known as **Boulle work**, developed. This type of enrichment is most commonly found on cabinets, tables and the top rail of chairs. Veneered surfaces were sometimes embellished with fanciful penwork compositions or painted

41 with either classical subjects or **bunches of flowers**. Other

39 typical Regency features included the use of inlaid **ebony strings**,

37, 52 low brass galleries and **vertical reeding** on legs and columns.

The origins of the Regency period used in its widest sense can be traced back to 1783 when the Prince of Wales commissioned Henry Holland to improve Carlton House which he had been given on his coming of age. Holland supplied a quantity of French furniture either made by émigré craftsmen working in London such as Dominique Daguerre or purchased from members of the newly impoverished French nobility, and about 1790 he created a sumptuous Chinese drawing-room furnished with pseudo-oriental chairs, pier tables and an exotic chimneypiece. This ensemble forms an important prelude to the later Regency taste for chinoiserie. The refined character of **Holland's furniture**

Mirror with carved and gilt frame enclosing a convex glass. About 1805.

Armchair and footstool. About 1807–1810. Made, probably to designs by Henry Holland, for the drawing-room of Southill Park, Bedfordshire. Collection of Major S. Whitbread, Southill.

left Tripod table on three monopodia supports. About 1810. Derived from a design by Thomas Hope. Formerly at Clumber Castle. Victoria and Albert Museum, London.

right Stool in simulated rosewood with gilt terminals based on a design by Thomas Hope. About 1808. Private collection.

35 **designs** is revealed most clearly in the pieces inspired by a personal interpretation of the Louis XVI style which he supplied to Samuel Whitbread's house at Southill, Bedfordshire, between 1796 and his death in 1806. He displays much greater awareness of contemporary French fashions than Sheraton and his main achievement was to infuse elements of French classicism into the native tradition, a development which exercised a formative influence on the character of later Regency furniture.

Henry Holland's assistant Charles Heathcote Tatham also played a key part in advancing one of the principal Regency styles, although he never designed furniture himself. Tatham spent two years studying classical remains in Italy and in 1799 published his well known *Examples of Ancient Ornamental Architecture* containing 'an accurate pictorial record of Graeco-Roman decorative details and many recently discovered examples of ancient bronze and stone furniture'. The volume did much to encourage a more precise archaeological approach to furniture design, for his illustrations of classical forms and motifs were rapidly assimilated and adapted by designers such as Thomas Sheraton, Thomas Hope and George Smith. During the early and 36 mid Regency period novel features such as **chimera** (a fabulous lion-headed goat sometimes having wings and a serpent's tail),

Grecian couch in rosewood. About 1812. Made by William Trotter of Edinburgh for Paxton House, Berwickshire. Collection of Mrs H. Home Robertson, Paxton House.

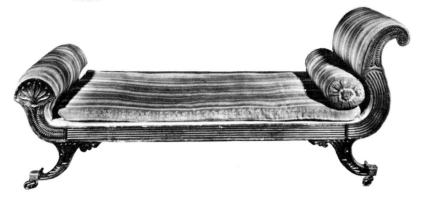

36 **lion mask with ring** ornaments, supports in the form of terminal
36 figures, circular tables on three **monopodia** (supports having
    the head and body formed with a single leg and foot), and **X-**
36 **framed stools** based on classical prototypes abound.

    The stimulus which Tatham's volume gave to the serious study of archaeological furniture marks an important new phase of Neo-classical art for, while Adam and his followers very seldom attempted to reproduce actual antique models, Regency designers consistently sought to base their forms on the remains from
40 classical sites illustrated by Tatham and other scholars. Adam wished merely to 'seize the beautiful spirit of antiquity and transfuse it with novelty and variety' whereas Thomas Hope and his contemporaries aimed to recreate items such as couches, tables, stools, tripods and so forth from antique sources.

    The first book of designs to reflect the new tendencies was Thomas Sheraton's *Cabinet Dictionary* which appeared in 1803 and was followed by *The Cabinet-Maker, Upholsterer and General Artist's Encyclopaedia* issued in parts between 1804 and 1806. Sheraton was unusually responsive to changes in fashion and later designs anticipate the principal stylistic trends of the next decade. His *Cabinet Dictionary* illustrates many pieces allied to the furniture which Henry Holland had supplied to Carlton House and Southill; he therefore introduced a sophisticated version of the classical French tradition to a wide audience of cabinetmakers and patrons. The influence of Tatham's *Examples of Ancient Ornamental Architecture* is also marked, and inspired many designs of striking originality. For example, Sheraton illustrates the characteristic **Grecian couch** with scrolled ends and lion's paw feet for the first time. Animal motifs derived from ancient prototypes such as **monopodia, lion's heads**, eagles and dolphins occur in many engravings, the standard inward-curving **sabre chair leg** and tables with solid **vase-shaped supports** also feature, together with comparable novel elements which were more fully exploited at a later date. Due to the mental infirmity from which Sheraton suffered, his last work, the *Encyclopaedia*, contains many highly eccentric designs. However his experiments in the Egyptian, Gothic and Chinese tastes signal the direction in which the Regency style was to develop.

Holland and Sheraton both died in 1806 and the following year the eminent scholar and architect Thomas Hope published his immensely influential *Designs for Household Furniture and Decoration*. Hope had visited many ancient sites in Italy, Greece, Egypt and Syria, studied remains in the principal European museums (notably Portici where relics from Pompeii were displayed) and owned an extensive collection of classical vases and sculpture. He drew further inspiration from the engravings of Piranesi and Tatham and his close friendship with the architect Percier familiarised him with the French Empire style. Hope's passion for archaeology governed his approach to furniture design, and he translated ancient forms with a skill which made Sheraton's efforts in the same direction appear very amateurish. Hope realised, however, that it was not always practical to produce replicas in wood of the massive stone furniture excavated at ancient sites or items portrayed on classical vases, wall paintings or in sculpture. He therefore compromised in the spirit of the great French designer Fontaine who wrote, 'We have followed the models of antiquity not blindly, but with discrimination entailed by the manners and materials of the moderns.'

Many of the designs in *Household Furniture* portrayed pieces

39   of furniture made for **Hope's house** in Duchess Street and, although the *Edinburgh Review* scorned his creations as 'an assemblage of squared timber and massive brass which would weigh down the floor and crush out the walls of an ordinary London house', he noted in the preface to his volume that imitations of his furniture had already 'started up in every

36, 39   corner of the capital'. The significance of **Hope's designs** is that they were widely acclaimed in fashionable circles and ushered in the taste for archaeologically inspired furniture.

       Among the most admired new types were small **circular**

36   **tables** or stands supported by three chimera monopodia; **centre**

39   **tables** with triangular pedestals; oblong tables with lyre-shaped or solid console end supports; torchères in the form of Roman

36   tripods; X-framed chairs, and **stools** and chairs with gracefully curved scimitar legs and curved back rails following precedents

Pedestal table in mahogany inlaid with ebony and silver. About 1810. Based on a design by Thomas Hope and made for his house at Deepdene, Surrey. Victoria and Albert Museum, London.

Design for a dressing table from George Smith's *Household Furniture* (1808), Plate LXXII. Based on an engraving of an antique seat of Roman marble published by C.H. Tatham in 1799.

in Greek vase paintings. Hope approved of severe rectangular shapes with broad areas of flat veneer sparsely enriched with ormolu mounts or **ebony inlay**. His decorative repertoire included anthemion motifs, acanthus leaves, Greek key pattern, the 'cracker' column with double-lotus ornament, caryatids, lion masks and paws and elements from Egyptian sources. Hope's ability to combine utility with aesthetic idealism enabled him to design useful furniture of great originality.

The Regency style as developed by Sheraton and Hope was fluently translated into vernacular terms by **George Smith**, whose *Collection of Designs for Household Furniture and Decoration*, published in 1808, served to stimulate and satisfy popular demand for ordinary household furniture reflecting the new criteria of taste. Smith was a practising cabinetmaker and did not aspire to the degree of archaeological correctness attained by the scholarly Hope; however he succeeded in adapting the characteristic forms of ancient Egyptian, Greek and Roman furniture to a wide range of domestic pieces and firmly established Hope's themes in the mainstream of furniture production. He also included a number of fanciful designs in the Chinese and **Gothic tastes** which were currently enjoying a revival. Sheraton had illustrated a few examples of these styles in his late works, but

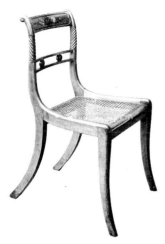

'Trafalgar' chair in satinwood with painted decoration on the top rail. About 1805–1810. Lady Lever Art Gallery, Port Sunlight, Cheshire.

Hope apparently considered them too frivolous to be worthy of his notice. Smith's *Household Furniture* therefore provides an admirable summary of the Regency style as developed by Holland, Sheraton and Hope. No equally comprehensive volume appeared until 1820; accordingly its influence on cabinetmakers and patrons was profound. During the interval the lead in publishing designs passed to Ackermann's fashionable monthly magazine *Repository of the Arts*–equivalent to the presentday *House and Garden*–which appeared between 1809 and 1824. Each issue contained a plate illustrating furniture in the latest smart taste by contributors such as George Smith, George Bullock, John Stafford of Bath and Pugin the elder.

Nelson's famous naval victories over the French account for the popularity of marine emblems in early Regency furniture and silver. Anchors, shells, cannon balls, rope, oars, telescopes, tridents and so forth were freely incorporated into designs, and in 1813 a splendid suite of dolphin furniture by William Collins was presented to Greenwich Hospital in his memory. Sets of supremely elegant **'Trafalgar' chairs** with **rope mouldings** on the top rail and back posts, caned seats and gracefully curved legs were made in large numbers for dining-rooms until about the year 1820.

41

Mahogany bracket clock in the Egyptian taste. Movement by Brockbank & Atkins. About 1810. Bank of England, London.

The Regency vogue for furniture in the Egyptian style can be traced to Napoleon's Egyptian campaign of 1798–1801, which ended in his defeat at the battle of the Nile. The French army was accompanied by a team of skilled archaeologists and artists under the direction of Baron Denon who published *Voyages dans la Basse et la Haute Egypte* on his return to Europe in 1802. The work was profusely illustrated with antiquities, and achieved immediate fame. Piranesi (1720–1778) had been one of the few decorative artists to display any interest in the Egyptian style prior to Napoleon's invasion, but his designs for chimneypieces and a weird scheme for the English Coffee House in Rome were either ridiculed or ignored by contemporaries. However, Baron Denon's volumes (printed in London in 1802) inspired a cult for Egyptian forms and ornament which received further encouragement in England from Nelson's historic victory. During the Regency period the style is perhaps best represented by small scale embellishment on such articles as **clock cases**, candlesticks and Wedgwood's popular *rosso antico* wares.

42

Egyptian style wine cooler in mahogany inlaid with brass stringing lines and sphinx feet. Lock stamped 'I. BRAMAH PATENT'. About 1810. Temple Newsam House, Leeds.

Thomas Sheraton, always alert to new fashions, introduced random sphinx heads, **sarcophagus shapes**, mummy feet, scarabs, crocodiles etc. into designs in his famous *Encyclopaedia,* but he handled the style with little assurance. Chippendale the younger supplied furnishings in the Egyptian taste to **Stourhead** in 1804–1805 and Hope illustrated an Egyptian Room in his *Household Furniture* of 1807, but neither attempted to imitate actual examples of furniture dating from the time of the Pharaohs. George Smith's designs reveal the same principle of applying Egyptian ornament to otherwise conventional Regency forms. Among the most common features were figure supports or colonnettes in the form of elongated mummy cases with ormolu heads and feet, carved lotus decoration, mounts imitating the winged sun disc emblem, bands of hieroglyphics, **recumbent sphinx feet** and the use of pylon and **sarcophagus shapes**. The vogue was at its height about 1810 and had become absorbed into general furniture practice by 1812 when the *Repository of Arts* published a number of Egyptian designs. Although its

43

43

44

43

influence persisted until the 1830s the first person to commission furniture closely based on ancient Egyptian prototypes was the Pre-Raphaelite artist Holman Hunt who in 1856 employed Crace & Son to make a set of chairs modelled on a stool in the British Museum.

The Regency period witnessed a lively revival of interest in the Neo-Gothic taste associated with Chippendale and Walpole which had been suppressed by Robert Adam's Neo-classical revolution. The style is not represented in Hepplewhite's *Guide* or Sheraton's *Drawing Book*, but Gothic elements reappear in Sheraton's second pattern book, the *Cabinet Dictionary* (1803), and his *Encyclopaedia*. Once again no attempt was made to copy

Mahogany library table, ornamented with philosophers' and Egyptian heads. Made by Thomas Chippendale the younger for Stourhead, Wiltshire, in 1805. The National Trust, Stourhead.

the structure of medieval furniture, Gothic details merely serving as trappings for modern design types. George Smith also provided

45 several engravings for beds, chairs and **bookcases** in the full Gothic manner observing that it 'admitted a more abundant variety of ornaments and forms than can possibly be obtained in any other style'.

The fashion was sustained by the historical romances of such authors as Clara Reeves, Mrs Radcliffe and Scott, and by the 1820s exerted a powerful influence on architecture and furniture. Its popularity is suggested by a contributor to Ackermann's *Repository* who in 1827 remarked, 'We have so many skilful workmen in Gothic that very elaborate pieces of furniture may

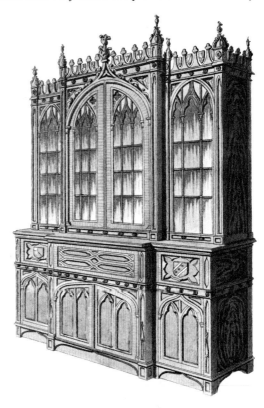

Design for a library bookcase in the Gothic style, from George Smith's *Household Furniture* (1808), Plate CIII.

be made at a moderate price compared with what it was a few years ago.' In 1829 A. W. Pugin's *Gothic Furniture* appeared illustrating a variety of designs in which medieval ornament was used at random—as it had been by Chippendale and earlier Regency designers—to create picturesque effects. However, Pugin's son Augustus Charles deplored such travesties of a rich traditional style and published his own volume of designs in 1835, also titled *Gothic Furniture* in which he sought to revitalise the essential spirit of medieval oak furniture. The younger Pugin made no attempt to contrive reproduction pieces but through serious study of medieval prototypes developed a historically sound style invested with the simple vigour, strength and sincerity of ancient craftsmanship. During the Victorian period his

Commode in simulated bamboo with Japanese lacquer panels. About 1802. The Royal Pavilion, Brighton (on loan from Her Majesty the Queen).

Chair in painted beech simulating bamboo. 1802. One of a set made by Elward, Marsh & Tatham for Brighton Pavilion. The Royal Pavilion, Brighton (on loan from Her Majesty the Queen).

reformed style of Gothic furniture was advanced by leading designers and the flimsy Regency version receded from favour.

The taste for chinoiserie associated with the Rococo style enjoyed a fashionable revival in England during the early 19th century. During the interval its expression was restricted almost exclusively to the field of japanning, chiefly on clock cases, and as an alternative to marquetry decoration on cabinet pieces. The Chinese drawing-room which Holland furnished for the Prince of Wales in 1790 anticipated the revival and paved the way for his designs for the Marine Pavilion at Brighton. The vogue in fact flowed directly from the Prince Regent's personal taste; it was primarily a court style and exerted comparatively little influence on the mainstream of furniture design. Inspired by a gift of hand-painted Chinese wallpaper in 1802 the Prince started to transform the dignified classical interior of his villa at Brighton into a sumptuous oriental pavilion. He equipped the rooms with bamboo furniture and bric-à-brac imported from the East by Crace & Son, moved the pseudo-oriental side tables and chairs from Carlton House to Brighton and contrived a suitably extravagant decorative scheme. Later, the firm of **Elward, Marsh & Tatham** supplied additional furniture in the Chinese style.

47

Several members of the court circle, notably the Marchioness of Hertford and the 4th Earl of Poulett, encouraged the mode and it was more generally favoured for bedrooms, but Regency pattern books, always a useful guide to popular fashions, suggest that it never enjoyed a large following. George Smith's *Household Furniture* for instance contained only four Chinese designs. Nevertheless, the Royal Pavilion is an impressive monument to Regency taste and certainly influenced the demand for sets of chairs of **simulated bamboo** and cabinets incorporating delightful panels of black and gold lacquer. The more exotic repertoire of Chinese forms such as pagoda roofs, mandarin figures, dragons, latticework and bells were used occasionally to enliven otherwise conventional types of furniture, and Chinese letters were expertly copied in decorative brass inlays.

The character of furniture as reflected in the designs of George Smith's first pattern book changed little until the years of the constitutional Regency (1811–1820) when there was a marked revival of the scholarly classical influence of Tatham and Hope and the end of the Napoleonic wars encouraged interest in the Louis XIV and French Empire styles. During this middle period the taste for furniture uniting refined proportions with austere classical decoration was overtaken by a movement towards more severe, massive shapes embellished with **florid antique ornament** or naturalistic motifs. The opulent French Empire style formulated by Napoleon's architects Percier and Fontaine was greatly admired in England and inspired a taste for palatial furniture richly decorated with ormolu mounts.

The Prince Regent's love of ostentatious display stimulated his interest in Louis XIV furniture, in particular the magnificent cabinets elaborately decorated with marquetry designs in brass and tortoiseshell. The Prince's taste led to a revival of **Boulle work** and created a vogue for furniture on French modelled prototypes.

During the 1820s several books of furniture designs appeared recording the final phase of the Regency style. Richard Brown for instance in a volume dated 1820 advanced a rather ponderous coarsened version of the vernacular Grecian taste while the

Grand piano in walnut inlaid with brass
Boulle work. About 1818. Made for the
music room at Brighton Pavilion. Royal
Collection.

Detail of brass inlay work on piano case
(see above).

Council chair in carved and gilt wood.
About 1813. One of a pair made for
Carlton House, London, derived from
a design by C. H. Tatham. Royal Collection.

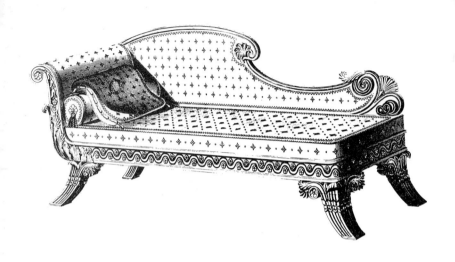

Design for a couch in Grecian style from
Peter and Michael Angelo Nicholson's
Practical Cabinet-maker (1826), Plate XXIV.

50 **Nicholsons'** *Practical Cabinet-maker* of 1826 emphasised the
trend towards virile floral and foliate ornament carved in bold
51 relief which superseded the fashion for formal **classical motifs**.
Another representative collection of designs was published by
George Smith in 1828 confirming that the sophisticated Regency
tradition had degenerated into a system of routine formulae and
insignia. Until the accession of Queen Victoria in 1837 the character of most furniture was still governed by classical principles,
but the chief interest of the 1830s centres on the emergent Neo-
Rococo, Elizabethan, Renaissance and reformed Gothic styles
which formed significant themes of early Victorian taste, a
subject requiring a further volume.

    Many designs in Sheraton's *Drawing Book* reflect the growing
52, 53 popularity of compact **dual purpose furniture** suitable for
small rooms, and during the early 19th century a variety of
mechanical devices were employed by cabinetmakers to meet

the demand. Between 1790 and 1830 over seventy patents were issued under the heads of furniture and upholstery compared with only twenty during the previous three decades. Thomas Martin writing in 1813 remarked, 'As it is the fashion of the present day to resort to a number of contrivances for making one piece of furniture serve many purposes it becomes necessary that the complete cabinetmaker should be acquainted with the principles of mechanics.' Most of the leading firms patented ingenious designs or bought the rights from the inventor.

52 **Morgan & Saunders** in the Strand were particularly well known in this field.

Armchair in gilt wood from a set supplied by Marsh & Seddon to Windsor Castle in 1828. Royal Collection.

below and opposite Regency style library
chair and steps combined. About 1810.
Made by Morgan & Saunders for Trinity
College, Oxford. Trinity College collection.

53   Collapsible **library steps** which converted into tables, chairs or stools offered great scope for novel constructions and **Harle-**

7   **quin tables** fitted with a rising till containing a nest of drawers which could be conveniently lowered to form a flat surface were made in large numbers—Sheraton illustrated and described the mechanism in great detail. Other typical space saving furniture included folding bedsteads that shut up to resemble a wardrobe, many different sorts of extending tables and reclining chairs equipped with adjustable backs, headrests, reading lecterns and footstools which lengthened to form a couch. Most patent furniture was designed in the latest fashionable style and pieces were seldom mere household gadgets.

The French wars stimulated the development of collapsible portable furniture with metal joints suitable for campaigns. Many patents were also granted for metal fitments such as locks, castors, iron bedsteads and for improved techniques for stamping handle-plates, knobs and other kinds of ornamental furniture mounts from thin sheets of brass.

The
Furniture Trade

By the middle of the 18th century there were probably over two hundred furniture workshops in London. The larger firms such as Chippendale & Haig, Vile & Cobb, Hallett, Linnell or Seddons generally combined the trades of **cabinetmaker**, upholsterer, interior decorator and funeral director. They supplied furnishings of widely differing grades suitable for either state rooms or servants' quarters and regularly accepted commissions to equip a new house with everything from curtains, carpets, wallpaper and chimneypieces to bell-pulls and even a simple chopping block for the kitchen. They employed large numbers of specialist craftsmen—carvers, gilders, chairmakers, upholsterers, marquetry cutters, glass grinders, metalworkers and so forth which enabled them to make furniture of much higher quality than provincial firms where less subdivision of labour existed. Accordingly, wealthy patrons generally employed London makers despite the extra cost of packing, insurance and transport; pieces for their less fashionable rooms might however be obtained locally.

Architects expected to be consulted about the character and arrangement of moveables intended for rooms which they had designed. Sir William Chambers for example protested vigorously when Lord Melbourne whose house he was building in Piccadilly neglected to obtain his approval of Chippendale's proposed furnishing scheme. Architects occasionally designed furniture themselves, but the majority merely advised patrons to commission drawings from a dependable London firm and might assist in making the final selection. An elegant group of such designs prepared by **Chippendale** for Sir William Constable of Burton Constable, Yorkshire, has survived, and a large collection of similar drawings by John Linnell and Gillows of Lancaster is known.

11

During the second half of the 18th century, many cabinet-makers established showrooms adjoining their workshops where the public could inspect their stock, purchase ready-made pieces or order special designs. For instance an entry in the Diary of John Spencer of Cannon Hall, near Barnsley, records that in the company of his architect John Carr he visited 'Cobbs, Chippendales and several others of the most eminent Cabinet Makers

'The Cabinet Maker'. Engraving from *The Book of Trades and Library of the Useful Arts* (1804).

to consider of proper furniture for my drawing Room.' As the century advanced a number of retail shops or Cabinet Warehouses were set up in London to provide an outlet for the furniture made by small firms and journeymen who did not have access to a wide public. However, there is little doubt that most of the furniture supplied to stately homes was specially commissioned and not bought from stock.

One of the tycoons of the London furniture trade was George Seddon of Aldersgate Street and a vivid account of his workshops occurs in the journal of Sophie von la Roche who visited them in 1786:

'We drove first to Mr. Seddon's ... He employs four hundred apprentices (and journeymen) on any work connected with the making of household furniture—joiners, carvers, gilders, mirror-workers, upholsterers, girdlers—who mould the bronze into graceful patterns—and locksmiths. All these are housed in a building with six wings. In the basement, mirrors are cast and cut. Some other department contains nothing but chairs, sofas, stools of every description, some quite simple, others exquisitely carved and made of all varieties of wood, and one large room is full up with all the finished articles in this line, while others are occupied by writing-tables, cupboards, chests of drawers, charmingly fashioned desks, chests both large and small, work- and toilet-tables in all manner of wood and patterns, from the simplest and cheapest to the most elegant and expensive.

'Charming dressing-tables are also to be seen, with vase-shaped mirrors, occupying very little space, and yet containing all that is necessary to the toilet of any reasonable person. Close-stools, too, made like a tiny chest of drawers, with a couple of drawers in, decorative enough for any room. Numerous articles made of straw-coloured service wood and charmingly finished with the cabinet-maker's skill. Chintz, silk and wool materials for curtains and bedcovers, hangings in every possible material,

Mahogany bed. About 1820. Probably made by Gillows of Lancaster. Formerly at Clifton Castle, Yorkshire. Temple Newsam House, Leeds.

carpets and stair-carpets to order, in short, anything one might desire to furnish a house, their own saw-house too, where as many blocks of fine foreign wood lie piled, as firs and oaks are seen at our saw mills. The entire story of the wood, as used for both inexpensive and costly furniture and the method of treating it, can be traced in this establishment.

'Seddon, foster-father to four hundred employees, seemed to me a respectable man, a man of genius, too, with an understanding for the needs of the needy and the luxurious, a man who has become intimate with the quality of woods from all parts of the earth, with the chemical knowledge of how to colour them or combine their own tints with taste, has appreciated the value of all his own people's labour and toil, and is for ever creating new forms.

Whatnot in mahogany with brass columns stamped 'GILLOWS· LANCASTER'. About 1815–1820. Collection of Mr Derek Linstrum.

'Two wishes rose within me. Firstly, for time to examine all these works, and then to see the tools with which they are made, manufactured in Birmingham, for I handled some of them here, and regarded them as most valuable and beneficient inventions.'

Viewed in retrospect one can discern a hierarchy in the furniture trade during the second half of the 18th century which started to break down during the Regency period owing to a dramatic rise in the population which encouraged semi-mass-production methods and the adoption of industrialised processes.

At the top of the scale were well known London firms such as Vile & Cobb, Bradburn, France & Beckwith, and William Gates who supplied the royal family, together with Chippendale, Linnell and Langlois. They were patronised mainly by the very rich (often on the recommendation of fashionable architects), made furniture of the highest quality and regularly accepted commissions completely to equip houses in the newest taste. Enjoying slightly less prestige were tycoons like George Seddon who produced an impressive range and quantity of elegant furniture designed for well-to-do customers which, however, seldom displayed the high technical finish and scrupulous choice of fine materials which characterised the output of firms in the first rank. Lower down the scale were numerous small concerns making competent inexpensive pieces indebted to the standard pattern book types, and finally there must have been numerous obscure workshops producing cheap utility furniture for the proletariat.

Although comparatively little is known about the work of provincial firms it is unlikely that any of them could rival the most eminent London establishments. Several, however, such as John Mathie of Edinburgh, James Cullen of Perth, John Stafford of Bath, Wright & Elwick in Wakefield, and **Gillows of Lancaster** were extremely proficient and secured the patronage of leading county families. Gillows were the most successful provincial firm and their output is probably fairly typical of furniture made in large cities outside London. It tended to be

57, 58

Details of impressed mark on side of the middle
shelf of the mahogany whatnot (see 58).

62   conservative and of **average quality** since it was intended for
local middle class customers who could not afford to employ the
foremost London cabinetmakers. However, payments to local
firms abound in the archives of great country houses and they
were evidently required to supply furniture for the less fashionable rooms.

     There were also hosts of country joiners producing chairs
61   with wooden or **rush-bottomed seats**, sturdy oak tables,
chests, settles, dressers, etc., in a plain traditional style for farm-
61   houses and cottages. Simple **country-made furniture** has a
sincerity and beauty rarely attained by more elaborate pieces
following the latest smart taste.

     When studying furniture it is essential to remember that
social and economic factors constantly exerted a powerful influence on design and that changes in style were seldom promoted
merely by the taste of a fashionable coterie. For instance the
custom of furnishing rooms on formal principles approved by
Robert Adam yielded in the 1780s and 1790s to a taste for more
casual arrangements providing greater intimacy and comfort.
Small occasional tables, stands and luxurious sofas became popular, and the new habit of dining around a single long table
instead of seated in small groups resulted in a demand for large
extending tables.

Fanny Burney, writing in 1801, observed, 'I think no room looks really comfortable or even quite furnished without two tables—one to keep the wall and take upon itself a little tidyness, the other to stand here, there and everywhere and hold letters and make the *agreeable*.' The introduction during the Regency period of **sofa tables, whatnots**, music canterburys, **davenports** and a variety of similar moveables which could be irregularly placed about a room increased the general impression of confusion which later came to dominate Victorian parlours.

34, 58, 62

Political factors such as the Napoleonic wars which reduced the value of money while raising the cost of labour and materials undoubtedly help to explain the decline in popularity of expensive decorative processes such as marquetry work or carving, and account for the large output of furniture having straight

Armchair in elm with rush seat. About 1805. Typical example of country furniture. Private collection.

profiles, plain veneered surfaces and turned members which were relatively cheap to make. The reason given by J. C. London in the preface to his *Encyclopaedia of Furniture* (1833) for the preponderance of straight legs on chairs and tables is that they were readily ornamented at a cheap rate on the turner's lathe, whereas all decoration on curved legs must be carved by hand at great expense. He noted too that the vastly increased demand for cabinet furniture in London was attended by a decline in the quality and design of furniture much of which became coarse and stereotyped. He also commented on the modern reaction against traditional concepts of simple elegance in favour of new-fangled forms and pretentious styles—many makers concentrated on tempting customers with novel, **over-ornamented** goods. These trends were fostered by such factors as the expanding lower middle class market for cheap, often vulgar products, the setting up of large furniture emporiums which waived the direct relationship that formerly existed between craftsman, designer and patron and, thirdly, new industrial techniques.

50

Davenport in mahogany with ebony strings, the top made to slide forward. Fitted with Stubbs patent lock. Made by Robert Snowdon of Northallerton in 1821 for a Mr Hayes. Private collection.

Trade label of Robert Snowdon
pasted inside the desk
compartment (see 62).

The population increase (9 million in 1800, 14 million by 1830) helps to explain the acceleration in furniture production and introduction of woodworking machinery. The turner's lathe which executed work impossible to perform by hand was the only mechanical aid used by 18th-century craftsmen. However, the machinery invented just prior to and during the Regency period was designed to carry out routine processes more rapidly and cheaply than skilled workmen using hand tools.

During the 1790s Sir James Bentham patented mechanical devices for sawing, grooving, morticing, rebating and moulding. In 1802 Joseph Bramah invented a contrivance for planing and thicknessing planks, and the following year James Bevan registered machinery to cut mouldings, reedings and other simple embellishments in relief. The power driven circular saw, mechanised fret saws capable of very accurate clean cutting and rotary moulding blades probably came into use about 1800 and saved much labour and expense. Patents were also issued for die stamping metal fitments such as handle-plates and mounts.

52   Although **traditional methods** persisted in smaller workshops, efficient woodworking machinery and semi-mass-production techniques certainly boosted the output of many large firms during the early 19th century. Sophisticated wood carving and dovetailing equipment did not appear until the 1840s and steam power was not widely used in the furniture trade until about 1860. However, the gradual transition from a craft into an industry started during the Regency period.

Acknowledgements

The illustrations on pages 46, 47, 49 (top and bottom right) and 51 are reproduced by gracious permission of Her Majesty the Queen.

The publishers wish to express their thanks to the owners of the pieces reproduced and to the following for supplying photographs: Norman Adams Ltd (photo Raymond Fortt) 31 right; B. T. Batsford Ltd 50; Bodleian Library, Oxford 28; *Country Life* 35 left, 42, 44, 49, 51, 52, 53; Fine Art Engravers, Godalming 47; R. B. Fleming Ltd 9, 24, 40; E. & N. Gibbs, London 34, 35 right, 45; Christopher Gilbert 62, 63; Michael Holford, London 4, 5, 16, 21, 25, 26, 29 right, 30, 31 left, 36 right, 58, 60, 61; Lady Lever Art Gallery, Port Sunlight, Cheshire 19, 41; Alexander Lewis, London 17 left; Radio Times Hulton Picture Library 55; Royal Pavilion, Brighton 46; Tom Scott, Edinburgh 37; Temple Newsam House, Leeds 2, 7, 10, 11, 14, 15, 17 right, 20, 22, 27, 29 left, 31, 43, 57; Victoria and Albert Museum, London 36 left, 39.

COUNTRY LIFE COLLECTORS' GUIDES

Series editor Hugh Newbury
Series designer Ian Muggeridge

Published for Country Life Books by
THE HAMLYN PUBLISHING GROUP LIMITED
LONDON · NEW YORK · SYDNEY · TORONTO
Hamlyn House, Feltham, Middlesex, England

LATE GEORGIAN AND REGENCY FURNITURE
ISBN 60043575X
© The Hamlyn Publishing Group Limited 1972
Printed in Great Britain by Butler & Tanner Limited, Frome and London